ISBN 978-1-913185-00-8

Published by Stan's Cafe
Birmingham, UK
2019

www.stanscafe.co.uk

Home Of The Wriggler © Stan's Cafe 2009
Photos © Ed Dimsdale 2009
Publication © Stan's Cafe 2019

Home of the Wriggler

a play by Stan's Cafe

Contents:

Home of the Wriggler	1
Bonus Material	
Programme Notes	46
Credits	47
Building *Home Of The Wriggler*	48
Walter Suett's Obituary	50
Griff's Story (full text)	53

Notes on the text:

Square brackets identify which performer is generating power on which device for which lights. Initials mark whose line is whose and multiple initials indicate lines that are shared.

Home of the Wriggler

Trev's Go-Cart
[Bernadette Wheel. LX DSL, DSR]

C   Now Trev works on security.
A   Trev, his father Stan and his uncle Frank all walked through B Gate together in 1969.
C   Stan worked in Assembly. Frank was a shop steward. Stan took early retirement. Frank stuck it out, he got a redundancy package.
A   Stan had made Trev's first go-cart from parts smuggled out of work.
Trev and his best pal Bobby tested it out on the Lickey's.
C   It was beautifully made, solid, with a Leyland badge on the back.
A   The boys were bounced about like rally drivers on the rutted paths, screaming and shouting.
C   Bobby worked at the plant in Logistics, left to work for a supplier in '89, now he's at the Chamber of Commerce encouraging, amongst others, the 'Creative Industries'. Bobby had moved away and Trev hadn't seen him for years.
A   Until he was there on the news.

Press Conference
[Heather Bike 2 LX A]

A	Bobby's grown used to public speaking at the Chamber but the media's different.
	He checks his raincoat, tie and hair very briefly before leaving.
	He swings the door. TV lights blaze.
	Flashes do their thing rapid fire.
C	"Ladies and Gentlemen of the media"
A	Bobby reads his prepared statement carefully,
C	"we are determined"
A	from the top step, word by word.
C	"best we possibly can"
A	The words are carefully chosen,
C	"to minimise the effect"
A	reassuring but realistic,
C	"funds are available"
A	no hostages to fortune.
C	"employees and the supply chain"
A	As Bobby reads, he tries to keep images of his childhood,
C	"retrain"
A	his family,
C	"re-skill"
A	friends,
C	"move forward"
A	and former colleagues at bay.
C	"ensure the West Midlands remains the manufacturing heartland of this country".
A	The statement closes and questions rain in,
C	"Thank you for your time".
A	an indistinguishable roar.

Trev On The Gate
[LX DSR, DSL]

A	Trev's part of the skeleton staff, on Security (a 'transferable skill').
C	He sits in a yellowing chalk white sentry box with a two bar heater

	and watches as another container marked up for China is prepared for haulage.
	Lorry gears mesh. Pencil stub tick.
	Trev snaps Dairy Milk and twists the radio up.
	He watches the lorry's driver spin with the heal of his hand, one way, then the other.
A	He pushes chocolate against the roof of his mouth with his tongue and feels it dissolve.
	He watches as the lorry pulls through the gates,
	pauses, indicating right,
	then red break lights off and away she sails.
	Trev swears to himself. He shouts out loud. He screams.
	He stabs the pencil blunt, flattened and snapped.
	His hand is bleeding.
C	April 2005.

Summary #1
[LX USL]

B	Ali is retraining as a plumber.
	Sanjay's newsagent is on the rocks.
	Dave hasn't slept well since Carol left.
	Carl is considering his options.
	Tony's popularity ratings are down.
	Akram is one sale off his bonus
	and the Mohony–Macraw merger is off.
A	February 1999.
B	Janice is off sick.
	Little Julie's eczema is getting worse.
	Lesley is covering for Beth.
	Sue and Desmond are trying to re-mortgage.
	Bill still writes to the council every day.
	Doctor Fenton is recruiting a locum.
	Ham and Varsha are trying for a second kid.

Alf, Jock & Kay
[Heather Bike 2 LX A & C]

A	Varsha usually works in the canteen, today she is in the conference suite.
C	Because Janice is off sick. Sinead...
A	Sinead is Varsha's supervisor.
C	Sinead is under stress.
A	Jock is late.
C	He's stuck in traffic.
H	There are road works in Northfield. No one's getting through.
A	Jock's 45, he likes a dram like his dad, Alf.
A	Alf worked in the drop forge for years. He came in by bus from the Black Country, bashed metal all day and got the bus back home.
C	Now he's half deaf and resident at William Hill. Alf is proud of his granddaughter. He thinks she is smart and beautiful. His wife once said "Kay, she has the most beautiful hair in Birmingham".
B	Kay is an air steward. She is flying back from Munich. Today she is looking after Business Class. She asks passengers to stow luggage in the overhead lockers provided or under the seat in front. A distinguished man with grey hair is her only eye contact. She's got a bottle of Bells in he bag for her granddad, Alf.
C	Katja once taught Kay at the Brasshouse but her numbers dropped and the course folded. Now Katja lives in Stuttgart with Ian and their son Wouter.
A	He's bilingual: Brummie/Schwabish. Wouter...
B	Vouter.
A	Vouter vould have shared a class with Julie and John if he had stayed. Julie's mum Linda is working on her certificates. She's a teaching assistant at Holly Hill where Julie goes. Doctor Fenton sent Julie to the Q.E.H.,
H	Queen Elizabeth Hospital, Selly Oak.

A	Where they scratched her skin until they got a reaction. Julie may be allergic to dairy products, but what's the alternative?
B	Soya.
A	Soya is an alternative to dairy products.
C	Julie wears cotton gloves at nursery. [Black Out] What have cotton gloves got to do with being allergic to dairy products? [LX A & C]
AH	Stops you scratching (eczema).
C	Right. John is becoming a handful. John's dad was John.
H	All first boys in John's family were John.
C	John was the fifth John.
H	He was Little John.
C	Little John was born three months early. He lay in a warm box fixed up with wires and tape. In the Q.E.H..
B	Susan was worried sick.
A	Susan was Little John's mum. John's wife. She carried John well.
B	Susan was tiny even when she was pregnant.
A	She carried Little John well.
C	But not long enough.
B	When Little John was born Susan cried a cocktail of drugs and emotions.
C	John didn't know what to say or do.
H	Little John was purple, transparent.
C	John went back to work. He had to.
A	He avoided things he should have dealt with.
C	He did his best.
A	He didn't try.
C	He worked hard.
A	He was selfish.
C	They had different perspectives.
B	Susan stayed as long as she could, deep into the night, her hand pressed against the perspex box.

Malcom Fancies Karen
[Amanda Bike 1 LX D]

H They were trying to call Malcom Nash because of his teeth but the nickname wasn't sticking.
Malcom sat in Carl Buxton's sex-education lesson. Someone had written "Seminal Vesical" on a desk and Buxton was losing it.
Malcom fancied Karen.
He didn't know Karen was pregnant – no one did.
Not even Buxton, who was bracing himself to discuss contraception.
Malcom looked out of the window, past the playing fields at a man walking his dog in the rain. He couldn't wait to leave school and start earning money.

Tony Thinks About Mary

B The agency sent Tony to R.K.Ferriss and Son.
C Founded 1947 suppliers of trim, washers and matting.
H Their regular driver did his back last week.
B "It's okay"
H He thinks.
B "Early starts, home by four. Regular runs. It's okay"
"Geoff doesn't take the piss"
A Who's Geoff?
C The boss.
H "It's okay"
Tony's waiting whilst the guys with the forks unload. Thermos coffee, Auto Trader, old papers, Galaxy in the background.
B "It's strange to be back. Look at this place, it's ancient."
H He did the right thing
B "I did okay"
H The pay off made sense.
B He knew it would only be going one way.
H He got out early on top money, took a lump off the mortgage and paid for the training and license.
B "The money will get better. I'll get off agency books, they'll always need haulage. I'll get a long term contract, get my own rig, start a business, lease one maybe, take

	on some other guys"
H	"mates, Johnny, Phil maybe"
B	"people I can trust. Gear it up"
H	"I'm good with people, I earn respect"
B	They made him a team leader young.
	That was a tough job,
H	taking shit from both sides.
B	"I did a good job here"
H	"It's reliability that counts"
B	"I'm reliable"
H	In most ways.
B	He should have sorted it out with Mary.
H	"That was bloody stupid"
B	He was stupid.
H	He should have said something.
B	Done something.
H	Whilst he had the chance.
B	Now...
H	working these hours...
B	it's difficult.
H	it's too late.
B	He never sees her any more.
H	"I never see her around"
B	It was a year ago?
H	Two?
B	Certainly before he left.
H	Whilst he still had the Carolla.
C	There's a hammering on the cab door.
	Paperwork to sign and "move her out!"
	[LX D off B on]
A	On the gate a security guard, pencil stub in hand, holds a clip-board aloft.
C	Tony's farewell salute.
	Left foot down, right foot up, across and down.
A	Red lights blaze.
C	Left hand out and back.
A	Yellow lights blinking.
C	Right foot up,
A	Red lights off.
C	across and down. Left foot up.
	Spin with the heel of the hand, one way, then the other.
A	Yellow blink off.

C	Left foot down, right foot up. Left hand out and back. Left foot up and right foot down. Right and right again. Right down the hill. First exit at the roundabout and straight on. Out towards the motorway. Walking beside the road, a woman, five foot 9, beige coat, dark hair.
H	Lonely female, 35, WLTM N/S male for walks and possible LTR.
A	Mature blonde, large curvy figure, seeks athletic man - any age - for good times.
B	Genuine 45-year-old, honest and kind, seeks someone to put the sparkle back in life.
H	Outgoing and bubbly 30-year-old, likes travel, WLTM easy going guy, 25-40, with GSOH for adventures and possibly more.
C	Lonely male, easy going, GSOH, likes cinema and walks, seeks genuine female for cosy nights in and possible LTR. [Blackout]

Johnny Kissing Mary
[LX D]

B   Johnny was kissing Mary last night.
H   He wanted more, but she said "no way".
B   Mary was kissing Johnny but thinking about Tony.
H   Tony was long gone.
B   Tony got out with a pay-off and is driving HGVs.
     Johnny was kissing Mary. He liked her.
H   But not enough.
B   She was born during the power cuts,
     delivered by candle light to Brian and Margaret.
H   Brian and Margaret were Mary's parents.
     They hired the Cross Keys pub for their Ruby wedding anniversary. Everyone was there. It was packed.
     They jived all night.
B   Brian died in 2000. Margaret still works in William Hill.
     Margaret's best friend is Peggy.
     She lives two down.
H   Peggy's daughter, Sam, is off to college.
B   She's doing Psychology.
H   Sam and Mary were close friends but not any more.
B   Eleven Plus split.
H   Exactly. Sam's younger sister Beth goes to school with Karen.
     Karen feels odd.
     Karen has her hand on her belly.
     Karen thought she was once before but now she knows she would have known. She didn't and she wasn't. Now she does and she is.
B   Karen's dad will be furious and her mum will cry.
     Carl's photo is hidden in her room.
     Heaven knows what Scott'll say.
H   Scott is Karen's brother. He's a Bluenose.

Scott: Football Thug
[Amanda Bike 1, Craig Bike 2 LX A,B,F,G]

B	Scott got mixed up in the wrong crowd at St.Andrews. They travelled the motorway network together, four of them in Brass Neck's Focus, scarves trapped in the back windows wriggling to get free.
	Three hundred mile round trips midweek.
All	Big kicks in small towns.
B	Their rep. grew and travel turned low-key.
	Darren's Golf,
H	No scarves, no anti-Villa sticker.
B	Sidestepping the surveillance.
ALL	Text ruck rendezvous.
B	Then Winson Green with mates from school.
C	"Time to reflect"
BA	Etcetera.

Akram Zips His Fly
[Craig Bike 2 LX C & E]

A	Akram zips his fly. Thumps the tap. Dunks his hands. One shake and he smooths his hair damp, leaning forward, gazing into his own dark eyes.
	He's good and knows he is.
C	"People don't want to buy a car, they want to buy an experience. Your job is to sell them that experience".

Ken At The Docks
[LX A]

A	Ken works in the Hang Chow docks.
	He wears orange gloves and guides containers down onto trucks.
	Heavy metal incoming from the UK.
	Ken has a bicycle locked in the rack.
	He is saving for a car.

Pal And Dilip At The Auction
[Craig bike 2, Bernadette bike 1, LX A,B,F,G]

B	Thursday, Pal and Dilip are at the Highgate auction with Dilip's brother Raj and his mate Kash.
H	Kash has five hundred pounds burning his pocket.
C	"You won't get anything but a heap of crap for that!"
B	Kash thinks that's okay for Raj to say.
H	"Fuck off Raj!"
B	Raj has a Y reg Civic parked up.
C	Kash has to take the bus to work and thinks that stinks,
H	"It smells man!"
C	in every way.
B	Pal and Dilip are there for the buzz.
	The streets are hopping.
A	Burger vans are steaming.
C	Private sales haggled under lampposts.
B	The auctioneer keeps the babble incessant.
C	Cars drive in, idle and are off.
A	Dealers wax decisive - nods and the catalogue twitch.
H	Kash bottles it.
B	Pal and Dilip play the joyride game.
	[LX A,F]
A	"BMW 3 series?"
H	"Yes"
AH	[improvisation]
A	"Ford Mondao"
H	"Yes?"
A	"You're joking, that's a Dad's car!"
	[LX E]
C	Jock's in Northfield, on the Bristol Road. Close but no banana.
	From his cab Jock can almost see the plant.
C	From his cab he can see the queue stretching away down the hill.
C	Fuming.
CH	Grumbling.
CHB	Ticking over.
C	In the back, despite climate control, salads are slowly perishing.
C	Fury is pointless, Jock reaches for another gasp.

Herbert
[Bernadette Bike 1 LX D]

A   1905, Albert equates energy with mass and the speed of light.
Herbert had grown frustrated working for Wolseley.
He wanted a fresh challenge.
He was looking for a place to build Austin cars.
He liked former printing works in the countryside, so he bought it.

B   Stay there, do the Lickeys.

Brian And Margaret
[Heather Wheel LX DSR]

C	From the Lickeys they look down on fields of cars.
A	Eerie, massed at night, squadron by squadron, ranked for invasion,
C	A mechanised unit all shades blue in the moonlight.
A	Henry with a twist.
C	Any colour, so long as it's blue!
	Brian lets go of Margaret's hand
A	and moves for her waist. She responds in kind
	"they look beautiful don't they?"
C	"Yeah, they do, but there are too many of 'em."
A	"What do you mean? I like them!"
C	"There are too many of them. They're not selling. It's the wrong time of year. No one buys a car in the winter. They'll be looking to cut production, you'll see, there'll be a trumped up sacking and we'll be out. Cuts production and saves on wages."
A	Margaret's not sure what to say.
	Brian suddenly feels stupid.
C	Sounding like his dad.
A	"I'm getting cold"
C	"It's perishing isn't it, do you want this?"
A	Brian tugs at his donkey jacket.
C	[Starting to take it off]
A	"No. I think I'd like to go home"
C	"Oh, okay. I'm sorry"
A	Brian lets go of Margaret's waist.
C	Her arm drops too.
AC	They turn.
C	Brian can't decide if he's gone too fast.
A	Or messed it up talking about work.
C	He can't decide if it's worth trying something on in the car with the heater on.
A	He wishes his car had a heater.
C	"No heater I'm afraid"
A	He couldn't afford it. It was that or the radio.
C	"You may still want this"
A	"No, I'll be fine, thank you".
C	She smiles.
A	She likes him. He should relax.

C "What station do you listen to? I can get Luxembourg on this sometimes"
[LX USR torches on turntable. Dance]

Mary In The Pub

B Mary looks at her watch.
Tony is long over-due.
Mary is getting worried.
She doesn't like being in the pub on her own.
She tries not to check her lipstick or look at her watch.
The jukebox plays Phil Collins. *Another Day In Paradise*.
Mary toys with her glass.
[Blackout]

Summary #2
[Craig Bike 2 LX C]

B November 1995.
H Andy is excited about his new job.
Joe's nan has been taken into hospital.
Charlotte's training for the marathon.
Craig's praying for the holidays.
Simon's split with Tim.
The survey's come back on Nina's house
and Radovan and Ratko have been indicted.
A May 1957.
H Elvis is all shook up.
Ken's been taken on as an apprentice.
Little Trevor's learning to swim.
Frank's leg is in plaster.
Barbara has just been born.
Stan's still basking in Villa's triumph
and Emily's lobbying for a washing machine.

Mini
[LX C]

A   1957, Paul-Henri, Konrad, Christian, Antonio, Joseph, Joseph, Lambert, Gaetano, Maurice, Walter, Jean-Charles and Johannes all sign the Treaty of Rome. Oil prices rocket. So Alec has been asked to design a small car. Lionel takes a prototype for a test drive "Great," he says "now build the bloody thing!" So they did. Eight years later they'd built a million and forty years later they were still building them.

The Shopfloor
[Craig Bike 2, Bernadette Bike 1, Heather Wheel, LX A,B,F,G,USR,USL]

B   "Keep your hands to yourself you bloody perv!"
A   Wini was part of the legend that taped Ralph naked to a pillar for letting his hands wander once too often in the upholstery department.
B   "Carpet tape all the way up. We left his bits free"
H   "They didn't seem worth it!"
B   "Apart from that he was a bloody mummy"
H   "Must have been murder to take off!"
B   "Ha! Serves him right, bloody perv"
A   "We didn't see him again did we!"
C   "Is that true?"
A   "Do you want to try it on yourself?"
C   "No!"
A   "So does it matter if it's true?"
C   "Okay, point taken"
H   "Wini's a grandma now"
B   "Would you believe it!"
C   "Congratulations."
B   "Thanks"
A   "It's Sean and Sean that are the next likely bloody lads."
B   "Drive over from over Weoley Castle way together, they're inseparable"
A   "Always call in at Sanjay's for papers, pop and porn then Clock On"
B   "And see how much they can get away with"
H   "How little you mean"

B	"Yeah, how little they can get away with"
C	"Do you know what their jobs are?"
A	"No, I don't think anyone does do they?"
H	"They're a laugh though"
B	"I'll tell you who does work hard"
A	"Who's that?"
B	"Patrick"
A	"Pat Foyle?"
B	"No, Patrick, Patrick Green"
A	"Oh yeah, does he still have three jobs?"
B	"From the old piece-work days"
C	"What?"
B	"You got paid for what produced you, piece by piece"
A	"In some places it really added up"
B	"We were in all the papers as the best paid workers in the country, except they didn't mention the days when they sent you home because there was nothing to do"
A	"Then you got next to nothing. Patrick bought a coach"
H	"He's still got it"
B	"Loads of people had two jobs"
H	"He still drives a gang in and out from Redditch each day"
A	"Then he does shifts as a mechanic doesn't he?"
B	"His dad got sacked from the plant"
A	"That's it, two days off retirement!"
B	"They spotted a set of factory spark plugs in the door pocket in his car. Instant dismissal."
A	"The security guard was a mate of his wasn't he?"
B	"He lost his pension and everything!"
C	"Some mate!"
H	"It's pathetic, there are crates of them over at the engine works, stock control's all over the place, no one's going to miss four spark plugs"
C	"You'd think they'd sell us stuff at the factory gate…"
A	"Well you wouldn't you"
B	"They say the dealers would object"
C	"It doesn't bother them at Cadbury's"
H	"Exactly! There are three golden rules Phil: no nicking, no fighting and no clocking anyone else in or out"
A	"Even if they're stood right next to you"
B	"Instant dismissal"
H	"Have you heard about Charlie Holden?"

A	"About his wife?"
H	"Yeah, he's on nights now and the guy who's doing his job at work on the dayshift is doing his job at home on the night-shift as well, if you get what I mean!"
C	"Poor bloke!"
A	"And you think he's not doing the same when she's off at work in the day!"
B	"I don't know where they get the energy"
H	"That's Dave, he's 'The Prof',"
A	"Professor Yates, they've given him day release once a week to learn Japanese if you believe it"
B	"He's a swot and a creep"
A	"Mathias is a Kraut, but he's alright,"
B	"He works like a bloody dog"
A	"Fixing the head-linings. Worst job in the factory"
H	"He's glad to be back,"
AB	"You're joking!"
H	"He gets splitting headaches when he's off work"
C	"He's addicted to the adhesive?"
H	"Exactly"
A	"Glue sniffer"
B	"Russ the super, used to be in the paint shop but he cause so much trouble there they moved him here."
A	"Now he's trying to make such a bloody nuisance of himself that they have to promote him out of trouble."
B	"Really he's after a driving job."
C	"What's that?"
A	"You take a car out for a drive each day clocking up the miles checking for deterioration, that kind of thing. It's a piece of piss."
H	"Exactly"
A	"Des is a good lad, he holds the scooter track race record,"
C	"What?"
A	"It's a race, round the track"
B	"On scooters"
A	"Obviously! Des doesn't care"
H	"He's mental"
B	"He's changed since he met Sue"
H	"That's true"
B	"Have you noticed he's doing all the overtime he can get at the moment?"

H	"Yeah"
C	"When are these races?"
A	"Whenever. It's about stopping the boredom"
B	"Some sections put on shows in the lunch break"
C	"You're joking!"
B	"No, they're only short ones. There are darts leagues and all sorts"
C	"What about the management?"
A	"Management? You won't see them"
H	"Bill's your only problem"
B	"He'll scream and bloody swear in your face about sacking you"
A	"It's his only tactic!"
H	"Tosser"
A	"He's got a Napoleon complex."
HB	"What?"
A	"He's short so he acts like the Emperor of France"
H	"Exactly"
B	"I can't remember him ever actually sacking anyone"
A	"He hasn't got the authority"
H	"He can make your life shit though can't he"
C	"What about the Union?"
A	"Which one?"
H	"It wouldn't come to that, but they're okay if you have an accident, that sort of thing"
B	"Who are you with?"
C	"NUVB"
A	"Same as us"
C	"We've got 2000 members here"
B	"Yeah, membership's one thing, how many turn up to the meetings?"
H	"The real power's here on the shop floor"
B	"Bet you thought we'd all be raving lefties"
C	"Not really"
A	"You shouldn't believe the papers"
B	"Down here, most guys are fundamentally more Capitalist than the management"
H	"They've got a noose up for Frank Price in CAB2"
C	"Who's he?"
A	"You're joking!"
H	"Since MDW came in they've lost money"
A	"That's not strictly true though is it"

C	"What's MDW?"
B	"Measured Day Work"
H	"It's true for most people"
A	"It's true of some people some of the time, for most people most of the time it's better"
B	"But no one's got the motivation anymore, they get paid just for showing up"
A	"They're exaggerating"
H	"Before, your own guys would lynch you if you stopped the track, now everyone's pleased of the break and it's Bill that's trying to lynch you"
C	"Whose the guy whose got the noose up for him?"
A	"Frank Price, a union official who helped bring in pay restructuring. Some of the guys are pretty angry about it but Frank's alright"
B	"Yeah, Frank's alright. He's a Communist but he's alright"
A	"He's one of us really"
H	"They offered him a management job once"
A	"Trying to bring him on side"
H	"He said 'no thanks'"
B	"He said 'no thanks, you can't ride two horses with one arse!'"
	[LX E]

C	It was hot as hell and dirty.
	You couldn't see down the way for the smoke.
	It was hot as hell and dangerous with it.
	It was a dirty stinking job and heavy.
	You worked all day, forty minutes for lunch and you came home knackered.
	[LX DSR]

B   **The Funeral**

They named the community hall after Frank when he died. The whole family were there when the plaque was unveiled.
They had a great happy–sad party.
Balloons, bunting and The Jive.
The funeral had been packed with friends and people they didn't know. Fi spent the day being told by strangers what a great man her father was.
She knew that anyway.

C   Jim would have been Frank's son-in-law.
They would have got on he thought.
Jim moved to Birmingham when he was 21.
He worked as a waiter part time to pay for his writing.
He liked the fact people made things there.
He met Fi after she split with Nick – Rick, after the rallying crash.

Rick And Steph #1
[Heather Wheel LX DSR,DSL]

A   Rick married Steph, who he'd know for years before he looked at her properly, as a woman and saw someone different and someone he liked. She was an English student.
She followed him back to Northfield when he got his first job. He did good work on the 75's rear break light cluster, apparently. That got him the Peugeot contract. She got a job on The Mail. He's freelance now, of course, so's she.
They have a double garage but park on the block-pave drive.
They want to fill the garage with trampolines and bikes and kites. For now there's a chest freezer, old paint tins, an old lawnmower and a barbecue.

Susan The Hairdresser
[Craig Bike 2, Amanda Bike 1]

B	Susan had been working at the hairdressers for six years.
A	Hair Today, Gone Tomorrow.
B	She started when she was at school. At the weekend she swept lost hair from the floor and made instant coffee for the women. They let Susan wash hair when she was fifteen. She kept her fingernails short but well shaped.
H	These days she files them at traffic lights. It calms her down.
B	When she was sixteen she started college. She did Hairdressing at the College of Food.
H	Now she wishes she had done Beauty Therapy as well.
A	They didn't offer that then.
C	That was '89, Shiatsu didn't come in until the early 90s.
B	She kept up the weekend work at Hair Today.
A	Barbara, the owner, liked her.
C	Barbara's husband liked her but Barbara didn't know that.
B	Susan suspected that
H	but never said and never led him on.
A	Barbara said Susan could become a junior stylist when she qualified.
H	"Thanks"
C	Susan thought that would be okay at first maybe but hoped it wouldn't come to that. College meant Susan had got to know the City Centre. Susan was wanted to work at a salon in town.
B	Now Susan has Little John to look after things had changed.
H	Susan grips Little John under the arms and lifts him high.
A	Cofton Park.
C	Leaves in the air. Leaves on the ground
B	Little John squeals.
H	Susan doesn't know what's for the best.

Abdul And Az
[Bernadette Wheel LX USR, DSR, USL, DSL]

C   Abdul knocks another hundredth on the chuck and flings a hand towards Az in the gantry.
H   "Okay Az!"
C   Lowering starts again.
H   "Keep it coming"
C   He's been doing this job since he was 20.
H   The Gharwar oil field was discovered in 1948, it was the biggest in Saudi Arabia. In 2005 it produced over 5 million barrels per day, more than 6% of the world's supplies and no one could agree how much was left. It's crazily hot, the dirt and overalls make things worse.
H   "Az"
C   Abdul wonders if there's a better job for him.
    He weighs up job security against discomfort and danger. He considers his responsibilities as a father, husband, uncle, son. Change is too risky. These risks are better than those risks. This heat counters that heat.
H   "Another meter"
C   He raises his right hand again for Az to pause.
H   "Whoa!"

Rick And Steph #2
[LX DSR, DSL]

A   Rick and Steph have thrown a barbecue party.
    Rick thinks the barbecue is inadequate and wants one built out of brick with plumbed in gas. Everyone else seems happy.
    The new patio heater is working well.
    Everyone drinks as much as they dare; drivers and passengers, each to their own.
    They finish late and forget to turn the patio heater off. At five in the morning the gas give out and the flame dies.
    [Blackout. Break]

Mary At Work
[Amanda Bike 2, LX E]

H   Okay 3, 2, 1.
B   Mary glances at her watch. Countdown to a break. Peep in her ear. Auto-spiel. Corporate script recorded for training purposes.
"Hello Direct Line. Mary Speaking, how Can I Help You?"
Lonely hearts crossed and circled face down on her desk. Strangers in the ear all day, out of reach.
H   Colleagues harnessed mouth and ear, muttering to the ether. Quotes and claims.
B   She talks voices through on-screen menus,
"have you been refused insurance for any reason in the last twelve months?" return return return.
She warms to a friendly tone.
The system's running slow,
She flirts a touch in the hang time.
"That's a nice accent, where's it from?"
C   Raymond the supervisor is carpet creeping by the window, looking down at the street.
B   Mary toys with her pencil and jotter, sketching the face of the friendly voice cartoon chiselled and strong.
The system catches up with her, they're off and through and "Bye" and peep,
and here comes another.
"Hello Direct Line, Mary Speaking, how Can I Help You?"
The day loses shape.
"When did you pass your test?"
"Is that third party or fully comprehensive?"
"What make and model is the car?"

B   Rover 45
C   Rover 100
H   Rover 114
B   Rover 214 SEI
C   Rover 416i
H   MX3 1.6 0 3 fsh 9,500
B   MX3 1.8 v6 P reg MOT fsh 2195 ono
C   Clio 2.0 16v 172 bhp 2002 3 dr 17500 6750 ono

H	Merc 2.9 tdi 51 FSH 38k air con CD MOT
C	Austin, black, very clean, S-Reg, PAS, ABS,
A	GSOH, WLTM non-smoking Marina
C	must have R/C, MOT,and large curvy body, for outings and possible LTR.
A	Mature lady, new shape, air-bag, FSH, below average mileage,
H	WLTM easy going Rover 75, average build, for outings and possible LTR.
C	Handsome, automatic 28-year-old, looks superb, very clean throughout,
A	seeks non-smoking Princess, white with genuine low mileage,
C	£350 ONO.
B	Morris, K-reg, lovely condition, power assisted, 3 owners from new, WLTM reliable female with FSH and GSOH.
H	Must be good runner.
C	Part exchange welcome.
A	Genuine leather guy, immaculate, very nippy around town,
B	recently fully serviced,
A	seeks similar with new belts and brakes for fun and adventures.
C	No time wasters.
H	Clio, size 16
A	hatchback
C	has been around the block, WLTM vintage Cavalier with new plugs for travel and possible LTR.
B	Back to Mary she reads:

'Genuine guy, 25, caring and romantic, has been hurt in the past, WLTM lady, GSOH, any age, for cinema, walks and possible long term relationship'. She circles him.

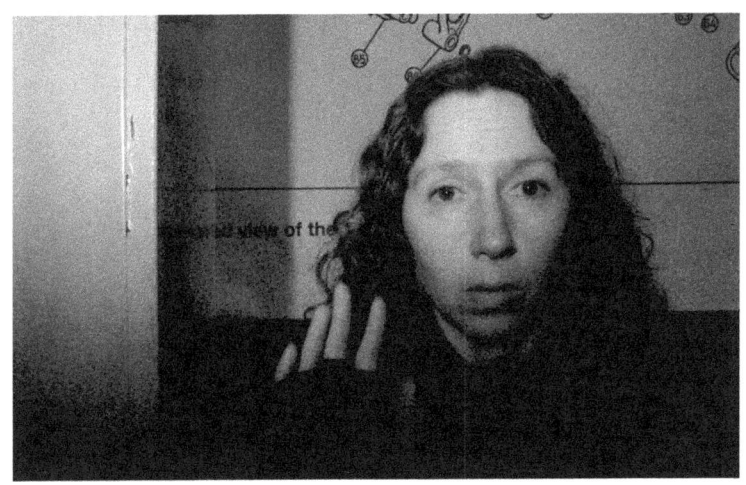

Akram's Sales Pitch
[Amanda Bike 2, LX A & F]

B	Akram is charming. Akram is friendly. Akram is respectful.
H	He anticipates and knows your life. He makes you feel good about yourself. He pats the buffed roof left-handed,
C	"Now this is a nice car"
H	He leans in conspiratorial, waves at the windscreen price tag,
C	"Ignore that, that's just a guide price"
B	He makes your deal sound special,
C	"I can have a word with the manager"
H	Akram can arrange finance,
C	"Don't worry if you haven't got the money now"
H	He will leave you to look round,
C	"Have a look around. Get in and out, pop the bonnet, check the boot, take your time, see what you fancy"
H	Right handed he motions towards the fresh coffee,
C	"Make yourselves at home"
H	He knows you want reliability,
C	"You'll have no problems with this".
B	He knows you want something that has a bit of oomph,
C	"It's a 1.8"

H	He knows you need space,
C	"You can add a roof-rack"
B	He knows you're after something that looks a bit tasty,
C	"Now this is a nice car"
H	He knows you're on a tight budget,
C	"You get a lot of car for your money"
B	He knows you're worried about French cars,
C	"I was too once then my girlfriend got a Peugeot, that was a lovely car"
B	He can wax lyrical about anything and turn on a sixpence.
H	He'll be just over here,
C	"I'll be over here if you need me"
H	He'll come and see how you're doing in a bit.
B	He won't be pushy.
H	He's never pushy.
C	"I can't sell you something you don't want. I wouldn't try"
B	He can do a special, special price but you must buy one…
BCH	today!

Rick And Fi In The Showroom
[Craig Bike 1 Bernadette Bike 2, LX B,F,G]

A   Fi and Jim are at the showroom checking prices.
H   Their Fiat's for it.
A   They want something with four doors, a small engine and some vague sense of get up and go.
H   They're broke but small ad. shy.
A   So they're here.
H   Jim's in the back of a 25, head crushed by the roof in a 'Buy British' vice.
A   Fi gazes across the hanger to the estates and V8s and major cash jobs.
H   Their salesman's doing his thing on another couple, the same thing, gesture for gesture, hand on roof, conspiracy lean, etc. etc., the coffee and leave them to wander.
A   The couple turn. Fi's right she did recognise that back, it's Rick, so the woman must be Steph.
H   Jim's by her side now.
A   Rick's on his way over, fake gregarious.
H   "Hi Fi, who'd have thought! Fantastic. This is Steph. Steph this is Fi"
A   "I've heard a lot about you"
H   "And this is?"
A   "Jim, pleased to meet you"
H   "You too… Rick"
A   "Jim this is, Rick"
H   "Wow, long time no see"
A   "Very"
     Easy so far but then the yawning years intervene and conversation stumbles.
     "Teaching"
H   "Living in Dorridge"
A   "Freelance design"
H   "This and that, writing"
A   "Journalist, freelance, Post and Mail"
     The split was so long ago. For Fi it feels like another life. She looks at Steph, an alternative her. Jim an alternative him. With a glow she realises she's happy it turned out this way.
H   "A run-around for Steph. New Mini"

A	"Something that'll start in the morning"
H	"Rick fancies a people carrier, Lexus or something don't you"
A	"Oh, have you got kids?"
H	"No, not yet, you?"
A	"Due in the New Year"
H	"Congratulations"
A	"Thank you"
	So it ends, with empty talk of meeting up and barbecues and one of Rick's cards in Jim's wallet. [LX B]
H	Driving home in their 607 Rick and Steph are quiet, the ride is quiet, the engine noise is low, the steering wheel whispers through Rick's hands as the car straightens up, his driving is smooth and precise, the cabin heater whispers. "What are you thinking?"
A	"Nothing"
H	"Was it strange seeing her again?"
A	"A bit. Not really"
H	"She seems nice, and he does"
A	"Yeah"
H	"You don't wish things were different do you?"
A	"No, of course not"
H	"Then why are you so quiet?"
A	"I'm not."
H	"Rick, you are"
A	Rick flicks the CD player on. "I didn't like any of the cars there, did you?"
H	"No, I still think we should order a new Mini and choose exactly what we want"
A	He scrolls through the discs and tracks looking for something that meets his mood. "Maybe" The strings swell on all sides, music for films and car adverts. He ups the volume. He glances up at a plane climbing westwards through the blue sky. He turns to Steph and back. He checks the road ahead.

Summary #3
[Bernadette Bike 2, LX C]

A   September 2001.
C   Sungita's learning to drive.
    Darren's Golf is off the road.
    Beth's fallen out with Stacey.
    Sean's growing a beard.
    Sue's diet's gone for a Burton.
    George shuts down US airspace
    and Brian goes to church for first time in years.
H   June 2005.
C   The Ingrams have been burgled.
    Kay's engaged to be married.
    Amy's been taken into care.
    Meryl is waiting for her test results. .
    Ed's snowed under at Citizen's Advice.
    John's made the cricket team.
    Rose has stopped smoking but Harry hasn't.

The Scan
[Craig Wheel, LX DSR DSL]

H   Cold gel hits Karen's belly and she squeals.
A   Beth's there too this time.
H   Karen's mum wanted to come but Karen wanted Beth.
A   Karen's mum had freaked
H   was still freaking.
A   Karen's mum is freaking but secretly likes the idea of a baby in the house again. Karen's dad is...
B   They don't think about Karen's dad.
H   Kim laughs, and spreads the gel.
"I warned you. Now, are you ready?"
She twists the monitor to the girls a fraction more.
Black and white.
The scanner is in her hand, descending.
[Bernadette Bike 1, LX C]

A   Beth gasps and cries, "There she is!"
H   From the deep-sea static Karen and Beth see a creature rising: a baby.
A baby, perfect and mysterious.
A   Kim takes them on a tour, she introduces them.
Minuscule hands and feet.
Calcium shadows of legs and arms and hips and spine and skull.
She tells them she thinks it's a girl.
"They knew it!"
"They knew it all along"
They gaze at her face in the dark.
They look inside her heart.
They measure her.
They cry, they hold each other's hands.
They say she's beautiful and repeat themselves.
H   She's beautiful. She's beautiful.

B   I love that bit.

Carl Waiting For Death
[Amanda & Heather use torches]

A	Carl is in the Xanthia.
H	Carl is in his Xanthia on the M5 broken down in the rain.
B	Assistance should be on its way. He called from his mobile, way back.
H	He knows he should be out of the car.
A	He knows he should have scrambled up the embankment.
B	He shouldn't be here.
A	He should be looking down on the motorway, the hard shoulder and his car from above.
H	Instead he is inside the car
A	as it is rocked side to side by the wall of air and sudden vortex of each passing lorry.
B	He shouldn't be here
H	in this delicate, thin metal shell.
A	The artics are just inches away as they roar through the spray and the night.
B	He should never have got himself into this position.
H	Carl knows he shouldn't be in the car.
B	He shouldn't be here.
H	He can feel his vulnerability
A	but he can't make himself leave.
B	He's trapped
A	and he can't help but hope that in one of those artics someone's taco will have shorted
H	and that someone will have driven too long through the dark and the spray without a break.
A	That now someone will be thinking of something else
H	someone else
B	Karen and the baby
A	and be letting their head loll in a cab
H	where the blowers are turned up
AB	too warm
H	and that
HA	twenty seven tons of truck
H	travelling at
HA	fifty eight miles per hour
H	is slowly
AH	veering off across a rumble strip.

B	It's out of control.
H	and with each mounting roar Carl
AH	braces himself
B	and prays for the impact,
B	the sickening pile-driving lurch of truck, coming through hatchback, rear crumple zone, seats and him,
A	concertinaing the whole thing together, fusing him with his engine
H	and wiping him,
B	his sorry life
A	and no-mark car
A	off the hard shoulder;
B	a smear of Autumn Roadkill.
AH	His eyes are closed.
B	He is crying.

Waiting For Jock
[Craig Bike 1, Bernadette Bike, 2 LX A,B,F,G]

C	Sinead's doing her nut. Varsha's finished the table laying. Napkin's origami starched. Place cards in place: Melberg and Byers. Mark and Tess will be in in a minute to finish off the last of the glasses. There's no sign of Jock, so there's little to serve. Melanie should be doing her nut, but as she says,
H	"I can't cook what's not here"
C	It's not her fault the delivery's not turned up.
H	"It's not my fault the delivery's not arrived"
C	She's prepared to make sandwiches.
H	"I could make sandwiches"
C	Varsha suggests she goes to Safeway in her car to get what's needed.
H	"That's a good idea"
C	Sinead isn't sure how that will be paid for
B	"We'll sort it later"
C	but they can sort that out later.
B	Mark bets Sinead £10 they won't be ready in time "You're on!"
C	Varsha takes a scribbled list in one hand, her coat in another and heads to the door.

Harry And The Taxi
[LX A,B,E,G]

B   Denise is at her post in the Arrivals Hall ready to see the Business Class - Hand Luggage Only brigade burst in from Munich. All men. Mostly suits. Some smiles. Passports held open, softened with use.

H   Harry knows he will recognise Professor Milberg but holds the card none the less. The greeting is polite, respectful and distant.
Handshake and thin smile, no more.
Harry decides to skirt the city.

A   A long route but fluid.
B   Views of the countryside.
A   M42, A441, Longbridge Lane, left into Q-Gate
B   Mr. Milberg looks over papers in the back.
H   Harry glances back occasionally in the review mirror.
It's been a long journey he thinks.
B   Ian and Russ have suggested Harry come in on a taxi with them.
A   He'd take one of the shifts and a third of the investment.
[LX B & E]
B   They'd keep the thing running 24 hours to spread the costs.
H   "I don't know"
A   It seemed a sensible idea.
H   "It's a lot of money up front"
B   Maybe he'd take the night shift,
A   concentrate on airport runs, avoid Broad Street.
H   "Isn't insurance a killer?"
B   Night driving, clear roads,
A   neon, sleepy passengers,
B   thinking time, free days,
A   nocturnal and opted out.
H   "I'll think about it"
B   He will ask Rose when he gets home.

Mike And Hayley
[Heather Wheel, LX USR, DSL]

A	Mike is a printer's rep,
C	Astra Estate a mess, samples: paper and finishes, old jobs, folders, proofs, paper cups, chocolate wrappers, hands-free cradle, notepads, Deluxe A-Z on the dash. He clocks up the miles,
A	all urban stuff, out to clients and back, picking up jobs, quotes,
C	occasional drops "Keeping things going, keeping people happy". It used to be a doddle,
A	a few regular high-run clients underpinned things, everything else was a bonus.
C	Now computers had blown all that out of the water. "It's a stress. It's all a stress" Now he genuinely does have to work late.
A	Barbara's hairdressing business was there for the extras, now it holds their finances together. They talked overheads. He even suggested Barbara let Susan go. He still fancied her but she'd started being funny with him since the salon's Christmas Party last year.
H	"She's pregnant now, it's clearly serious with this John"
A	Barbara said.
C	"It's a stress. She doesn't listen to me and I'm just trying to make it work. She doesn't appreciate what's involved."
A	"I know"
C	He knows these streets like the back of his hand, industrial sectors, trading estates deserted at night.
A	He's picked Hayley up a few times before. It's comfortable with her now.
B	She calls herself Hayley at work, her real name's Sally.
C	This works well for him here overlooking the canal.
A	"Here again?" Mike releases his safety belt. He pulls the bar up and pushes the seat backwards with his heels. He turns the inside hand wheel reclining his seat. He makes sure his coat is unbuttoned and open.
C	"It's just a little time for myself, a chance to think about nothing but myself for a change." A few moments of uncomplicated pleasure. [Blackout]

Carl And Paul
[Amanda & Heather use torches]

B	Amber flashing in the Xanthia rearview, drawing in close but slowing. Stationary. Cockpit light. Still lorries pummel the night. Off-side door opens and closes. Lime yellow fluorescence Grizzly bear gait Paul at the window. Carl leans across and winds.
A	"You shouldn't be here. You should never stay in the vehicle"
B	"I know, I'm sorry"
A	"It only takes one idiot"
B	"I know, it's the weather"
A	"Yeah, I've known better. No harm done. What's the problem?"
B	Paul is there to help. Carl feels sick. Carl describes the symptoms; the shaking, lack of responsiveness, his loss of control and power.
H	Paul listens concerned, sympathetic, professional. First find the fault. 'Ask yourself a series of questions. Is noise evident? Is there too much pressure? Make sure you have all you need to hand. Unscrew the lock bolts. Is air present? Is the breath restricted? Check for wear and distortion, adjust. Slacken, disconnect and release. Check connections and turn for support. Clean away dirt. Re-connect using new.'
A	"You start up, I'll follow you with my hazards until you are up to speed"
B	Carl thanks Paul. Paul has been polite and efficient. Kind. Carl has no excuse now. His car will take him home.

Karen In The Loo
[Craig Bike 1, LX D,G]

H	Karen's been to the loo, again. A woman is already there washing her hands. Karen shuffles up beside her.
B	They both look a little crazy; blue smocks and bellies,
H	Cream surgical stockings, no jewellery or make up.
B	"How are you bab?"
H	"Scared"
B	"Me too. This your first?"
H	"Yes" Karen smiles despite herself.
B	"My fourth, first C-section though"
H	"Mine's breach"
B	"Mine too, little bugger! Do you know what it is yet?"
H	"She's a girl, Chloe"
B	"That's a nice name"
H	The woman…
C	Pat
H	…drops paper towels in the bin.
B	"Well, good luck Chloe, you be nice to your mum. Good luck to you too bab. You're young, you'll be fine"
H	"Thanks"
B	The woman shuffles out before Karen can think of anything more to say.
H	She stands in front of the mirror, alone, pale in the flat neon light, She rubs the smooth hard lump under her ribs with her left hand. "Come on Wriggler. You heard what she said, we'll be fine" [Amanda on wheel, LX USR]
C	'Throughout England there were icy roads in the morning and fog that persisted in the South West. A northerly wind made it feel colder. High-sided vehicles were advised to pull over. Cloud increased later, there was patchy rain. Numerous hurricanes swept the South East coasts, they caused flooding and damage to property. Drivers were advised not to travel unless it was absolutely necessary. A factory fire closed the M1 from Junction 6 to Junction 12. All the roads in the vicinity were grid locked. A huge

wave hit thousands of miles of coastline. Traffic backed up in both directions and slip roads were expected to remained blocked for some time. An earthquake shook the East. Traffic light refurbishment on the Warwick Road caused hold ups on the Warwick Road and the Fox Hollies Road junction in Hall Green. 50 million people were affected by sudden blackouts in the North East Seaboard. The A460 in Staffordshire suffered lane closures at the Wolverhampton junction in Featherstone, because of resurfacing. 80,000 people died. No reason was given.'

Milberg's Meal
[Craig Bike 1, Heather Bike 2, LX A,B,F,G]

A	Jock and Varsha arrive at the conference suite simultaneously.
H	Jock's tail lift is down, trolley rumbling.
C	"Sorry love, it was a bloody nightmare in Northfield!"
B	"It's been a bloody nightmare here an' all"
H	Varsha's Metro is 80% foodstuffs.
A	"What the hell do I do with this lot now?"
H	Sinead doesn't know.
B	"I don't know, bring them in I suppose. More for Melanie to work with"
H	"What do you expect me to do with this lot?"
B	"Use what you need then we'll decide"
C	"Food for the troops!"
H	"Shut up Mark!" Mark is hungry and has been driving everyone nuts.
C	Melanie's all action
H	"It would help if you could prep some of this?"
C	All hands are on deck. Camilla's down from PR checking how everything is,
A	"All set?"
B	Stupid question, thinks Sinead surveying her frantic catering staff. "How long have we got?"
A	"The driver has just called to say they're ten minutes off. Then it depends whether Professor Milberg wants to eat first or look around."

H	"Let's hope he wants to have a good look round"
C	"Great impression we'll make"
HB	Shut up Mark!
A	To everyone's relief their guest wants to wander round the factory to get a feel of it before he sits down to eat.
C	By the time the executives sit down everything is ready and Sinead has won her bet.
A	She stands by the flapping door hoping to catch a glimpse of the German.
B	"What's he like?"
A	"Nice, handsome, in an old way, you know., silver hair, slim, steel rim specs."
C	"Distinguished" Tess adds.
A	"That's it, definitely. Distinguished."
B	"Has he mentioned the food or the room or anything?"
H	"He can have no complaints"
A	"No, he's just been talking and eating"
C	"He's not here for the food"
A	"He's polite enough though"
	[LX E]
H	Fifteen months later...
A	May 9th, 2000.
H	Milberg is back in Munich and John drives himself through cheering crowds at Q-Gate in a Silver Rover 75. Sinead and Melanie are putting the finishing touches to a small buffet.
C	Melanie says if she'd known the company only cost a tenner she'd have bought it herself.
	[LX A, B, G]
A	Sinead says she'd have gone halves with a fiver.
C	Five years later the Phoenix flame dies and they're doing agency work,
A	often together,
C	the cricket ground, The Belfry, big dos at the Holiday Inn,
A	occasional evenings at The Villa
C	and Perry Bar Dog Track.
A	There's variety and sometimes it pays okay,
C	but it's unreliable and there's no sick pay.

Bill Walks His Dog
[LX C, Craig stands on chair for backlight with E]

B   It's raining. It's scrubland behind the school, Bill Evans is walking his dog.
H   The dog's a mix, lurcher/whippet thin hair plastered to its ribs by the rain.
A   Chris is here to meet him.
B   A surprise reunion.
A   He heard about Bill's walks and is here to greet him.
H   Jane told Chris not to bother, that he wasn't worth it,
A   but Chris has had time on his hands.
B   Bill flinches when he sees Chris approaching.
    Out of context he doesn't know how to conduct this meeting.
A   The old threats hold no power any more.
B   The rules are different on scrubland behind a school. He holds the coiled lead more tightly and glances around for Princess.
H   She's off and away.
B   To call her would be to lose face, but he wishes she were at his side now.
A   Chris thought this would be easy, that the sight of his old supervisor would be enough, that the old adrenaline and suppressed fury would make it all too easy,
    but looking at Bill now all he saw was an old man in a faded car coat, stripped of all status, eking out time and money wandering the back ways, too old to start again. Eye contact.
B   Now they are yards apart someone has to say something; "Morning".
A   Chris just nods acknowledgement and keeps on walking by. He feels like an idiot. He can feel himself blushing for the first time in years. As if Evans would think he just happened to be passing this way!
H   Jane was right.
A   In some ways he was right, but he does have to set Dan an example. He is still relatively young. It's time to move on.
    [Lights are moved, improvised text about lack of decent lights]

Summary #4
[Bernadette Bike 1, Amanda Bike 2, LX E]

H   December 2009.
A   Brass Neck's two points off a driving ban.
Dilip's working for his Dad.
Tony's full time with Parcel Force.
Rick and Steph are living in Vancouver.
Sally's stopped calling herself Hayley.
Trev's at Merry Hill on Security.
Susan still works for Barbara, who's divorced.
Mary's on holiday in Spain and happy.

Griff's Story
[LX C,D,E]

H   Chloe's Grandfather was Ted, but his mates called him Griff.
C   Griff was a hard nosed bastard from CAB2,
H   according, to his supervisor,
B   Bill.
H   Griff didn't care what Bill said, he knew his sort, he knew his rights, he knew his value, he knew the value of the work he did and he knew when someone, Bill, was looking to set him off.
C   Fighting at work? Instant dismissal? No chance! Played right he'd be here until retirement on good money.
H   Griff was smart. Good money attracted smart people to dull jobs when Griff was making his way. Thirty years later he got his redundancy letter like the rest.

[LX D]

A Dear Mr Bateman

MG Rover Group Ltd is in administration. As you are aware I was appointed administrator on the 8th April 2005 together with my colleagues AV Lomas and IC Powell.

Due to the company's insolvency, it is with great regret that I give you written notice on the company's behalf that your employment is terminated with immediate effect from the 17th of April 2005.

The reason for your dismissal is that you have been made redundant.

I would advise that you should sign on for any employment or social security benefit to which you are entitled.

If you do not do so, the amount which you may be able to claim for the early termination of your contract may be reduced.

I will make arrangements for your P45 to be forwarded to you as soon as possible. Any claims you may have for unpaid holiday pay or pay in lieu can, within certain limits, be paid by the Department of Trade and Industry under the provisions of the Employment Rights Act 1996.

I therefore enclose form RP1 as supplied by the DTI for your completion. It is to be returned to MG Rover Group's headquarters as soon as possible.

RJ Hunt   Joint Administrator

[LX C,D,E]

H   Griff didn't want Chloe to be conceived,
C   but now, aged seven, she was part of his life, a force of nature.
H   Most nights Sandra and Karen would be out together,

both working late shifts at Morrisons. Morrisons weren't interested in Griff, Griff wasn't interested in them, a mutual repulsion that left him baby-sitting tonight.

A Chloe had grown up bright and secure, stocky and opinionated, a charming, pigtailed motormouth who had stayed up too late and was now demanding a story, The Story, in her small bed in her mum's room, from her Grandad. This is the story Griff told that night:

C "This is a legend from the future about the past in which a small girl takes ashes from the air and turns them into diamonds.

In this legend the girl wins trials of strength and cunning to bring all the world's jewels together for a year and in that year, using these jewels and the rays of the sun, she draws from the wind all the poison of the sky and forms it into the most breathtaking diamond necklace imaginable; a necklace that outshines all other jewels and sparkles as though all the stars in the sky had been set in a silver chain.

Although beautiful, people come to feel uneasy in the presence of the necklace. They claim that in its dazzling flashes they see great fires and furnaces, explosions and destruction. The girl knows these carbon visions are locked safe in the necklace forever but she is given an ultimatum – to relinquish the necklace or be banished from the kingdom. So, in a raging storm, she climbs a chalk path to a cliff top way above the sea. There, buffeted by thunder and etched out by lightning, she takes the necklace from her neck and hurls it with all her might up and out into the rain where she watches it spin and arc down and down until it is consumed by the surf and drawn from the shore by the waves. It sinks and nestles in sludge on the seabed. Where, over time it is covered by layers and layers of sludge.

It is said that even when this legend was last told, way in the future, the wonderful necklace still hasn't been found"

H	Chloe was told this legend dozens of times through the years, with minor variations.
B	It was her favourite, the only one that didn't come from a book,
H	the only one that could be told with the lights out.
C	Griff died in 2017,
B	when Chloe was twelve.
H	She remembered the story and told it to her girls when they were young. She tried to find where it had come from but she couldn't and eventually came to think what she had thought before, when she was young, that her grandfather had made it up.
C	It was the kind of thing he might have done,
B	but he didn't and he hadn't.
C	Three months before Chloe was born Griff had been interviewed about his old job by a theatre company and two months later he had been invited to see their play. It was full of half finished stories and the lighting was too dim. He wasn't sure what to think.
H	It wasn't his story after all, but this legend had been in the show,
B	right near the end.
H	It was near the end and as he travelled home he thought about the show, thought about the legend and thought about Chloe, the Wriggler and thought that maybe he would tell it to her when she was born.

[Torches & Music, lights reset for next show, improvised text ends shift.]

Programme Notes (2010 re-tour)

Home of the Wriggler was provoked by the passion unleashed in Birmingham when BMW announced it was looking to dispose of MG Rover. It was to have been a documentary about a working factory but events caught up with us; Longbridge closed within a month of our first research visit. It would have been easy to make this show nostalgic or a requiem for the plant but it's not our history to be that intimate with, so we have tried to steer clear of sepia images.

This show doesn't attempt to tell the story of Rover. Instead it tells dozens of human stories, some very short, some entangled, others standing alone; all start after their beginning and finish before their end, missing out on much in the middle. No one is expected to follow all of the show's strands, but we hope that in the collage of all these small stories, elements of a larger story will emerge.

Last year, with car production grinding to a halt around the globe, Detroit's 'big three' motor manufactures seeking vast financial bail outs and alarming new reports of climate change being published, the show felt urgent again and was revived

Although most of the material in *Home of the Wriggler* arises from stories we have been told, these sources have been mixed, mashed and re-imagined so that any resemblance to any characters living or dead should be considered un/happy chance.

The show contains a small amount of 'industrial language' and due to the vagaries of pedal power lighting levels will fluctuate in a mild strobing effect.

James Yarker.

Credits

Dedicated to
Archie, Eve, Jacob, Robin and their future friends.

Devised by
Heather Burton - Amanda Hadingue - Bernadette Russell
Craig Stephens - James Yarker

Performed in the UK by
Heather Burton - Amanda Hadingue - Bharti Patel (revival)
Bernadette Russell - Craig Stephens

Performed in China by
Amy Anne Haig - Bharti Patel
Bernadette Russell - Craig Stephens

Text - James Yarker

Devices, Design and Costumes - Mark Anderson and Helen Ingham.

General Manager - Charlotte Martin
Advisory Producer - Nick Sweeting
Photographs - Ed Dimsdale
Media & PR - Sharon Kean

Thanks to
Michael Martin - Walter Suett - Tony Williams for interviews
and others we know for fragments of their stories.

The Stan's Cafe Board
Peter Fletcher - Gerv Havill - Alan James - Andy Parsons
Roxanne Peak-Payne - Sadie Plant - Heather Taylor
Neville Topping.

Made with funding from Urban Fusion and Arts Council England.

Building Home Of The Wriggler

We made *Home of the Wriggler* in some terrible shell of a room behind a disused shop unit across the road from our office in Birmingham's Jewellery Quarter. Our office was north facing and single glazed with white emulsion breeze block walls. It was cold but the rehearsal space was something else again. There was no heat and no running water. We huddled in a side room making plans and moved into the main rehearsal room only at the last possible minute. All rehearsals were conducted in full-on 'parka' coats and gloves. The show was set in some post-apocalyptic future and we seemed to have got 'method' on this aspect of the show. Layers of warm workwear became the costumes; the actors just refused to take them off.

Originally it had been envisaged that the show would be devised by the cast but improvisations and all other known methods didn't seem to be getting us anywhere. The one solution appeared to be for me to sit down and write material which the cast could then play with and we could edit as a collective. The influence may seem ludicrous given the contrast in content but around this time we were all up all night every night reading James Ellroy's L.A. Quartet. I was gripped by the propulsive narratives but also revelling in his writing style with it's boiled down punchy sentences and absurdly, this script was my response.

I'd been harbouring the idea of a pedal powered show for years having, at the age of 17, seen Konstantin Lopushanskiy's 1986 film *Letters From A Dead Man* set in a nuclear winter where pedal power is the only energy source. A post-oil / post-car / global warming show seemed a good excuse to deploy this idea.

We commissioned our friends Mark Anderson and Helen Ingham to take on all design aspects of the show. Their solutions to our pedal power challenge heavily influenced how we staged the show. With two static bicycles and a hand cranked fly wheel used to generate power three acting positions were fixed. The lights were weak and the beams narrow so the actors had a small realm to work in. Halogen lights in tin cans on stands looking like microphones also dictated other acting positions. The actors play people themselves playing people and only slightly acting out these roles, so movements didn't need to be great, standing and speaking worked and the actors' physical efforts being directly linked to the light that allows us to see them proved a powerful device. Their breathing became strained by the effort of working the bikes and the power surge produced by each of the alternating downward pedal strokes caused the lights to pulse or to breath as if the show was set in the gloomy interior of a living organism.

Touring new unusual theatre in the United Kingdom has grown ever more difficult. One challenge is selling a show that hasn't been made for which there is no script, no photographs, no video and certainly no reviews. To sidestep this problem we planned to stage the show at two friendly local venues in early 2006 and use the momentum from these gigs to sell a wider tour. This plan worked moderately well as we eventually took the show out again in spring 2009 and to the Edinburgh Fringe Festival that August where it gained enough enthusiastic attention for some further touring in spring 2010. It's sad letting go of shows that you have a strong affection for but it seemed a fitting end when we got an invitation to perform the piece in Beijing in November 2010. *Home of the Wriggler* opens with a scene in which machinery stripped from the Longbridge car plant in Birmingham is leaving the site in containers bound for China to make cars there. It seemed fitting that our show would reach its conclusion by following the same journey.

And yet, Terminator like, it turns out that the machinery is not yet dead and scrap. It is hauling itself back together to tour again. Ten years after it last turned a pedal news of yet more car plants closing across the country, with yet more communities facing the difficult adjustment to a post-car plant world the show's time has come once again. It will be recast and restaged in 2020.

James Yarker November 2019

Walter Suett's Obituary

Five years after he was interviewed for Home Of The Wriggler Walter Suett died. This text, written for and read at his funeral by James Yarker, is included as it could easily have formed part of the show.

Walter John Suett was a solid man
He knew where he stood and what he stood for
And good luck to anyone who tried to shift him.

He was born into the back-to-backs of Barford Street in 1945
Son of Walter and Frances Suett
Bomb Sites were his playgrounds
A Satsuma for Christmas and two big bronze pennies
acid dipped to shine in the palm of his hand, as good as new
He would ride high, swaying on the woodman's stack of timber
A small boy boosted to sit astride Roy Roger's horse one night in the darkened stables.

A fledgling engineer building a push bike from scavenged parts
His father was strict, his mother strict Catholic
St. Mark's School combining the two
Here Walter met Tom and an epic friendship was drop forged.

Secondary School finished on Friday
and Walter started his first job on Monday
It didn't suit or stick but it taught him machine tooling
National Service took local lads to faraway lands
Walter saw foreign sights and served in Aden.

Hands on a gun, a small hand in history
Back home he walked through the gates of Austin Rover with his father.
He cut gears and, day after day, handed them to Ted
Another friendship welded: corrosion free.

Walter was always punctual - he was a Time and Motions engineer
Walter was a cautious driver - he was a Health and Safety officer
Walter was a man of principle - he was an elected Union Official
He rose through the union ranks to secret sandwiches at Chateau Impney
haggling new working practices for the workers in tumultuous times.

He was elected a councillor - overseeing Social Services
"Did I ever tell you of the Zebra crossing we got installed?"
If not once then two dozen times.

As Councillor he attended a tea party at Buckingham Palace before finally, as a sign of the times in Birmingham and beyond - Suett was replaced by Currie; Edwina was on the march and Walter was moving on.

He was plagued by ill health. As a child he suffered numerous serious conditions, including one which permanently damaged his eye-sight. His father died aged just fifty and Walter nursed his mother at their home on Central Avenue as she struggled against cancer and slowly died.

He took early retirement due to ill health, a move which freed him to do more work of the voluntary kind - twelve valuable years at the Citizens Advice Bureau helping people to gain control of their own lives, working with a team he respected and whose company he enjoyed.

Nineteen years ago Walter met Mavis and they embarked on a partnership that - despite Mavis insisting on wearing trousers and even occasionally driving a car - endured beyond many marriages. Walter loved Scotland and Italy and would talk of their holidaying together in those spectacular countries, but ultimately they always ended up closer to home with the dog, invariably it seemed choosing a fortnight destined to break British rain-fall records. They were sealed water-tight, a blessing.

You had to look carefully, but if you did it was clear that Walter was at heart an emotional, even sentimental man. Though without children himself, he cared deeply for them.

When governorships were introduced for state schools Walter, with typical commitment, took on five. In recent years he was proud to be associated with Albert Bradbeer and Frankley Community High Schools as their Chair of Governors and his extraordinary forty years of service in this field has just been acknowledged with an award from Birmingham City Council.

His pleasure in the progress of his honorary grandchildren was genuine and heartfelt. And his presents for them displayed both generosity and an uncanny sense of what young children would most enjoy.

Walter Suett was a solid man.
He knew his mind and wouldn't mind telling you what was on it.
He believed in civility, polished shoes and Marks and Spencer,
He liked history, biography, war films and cowboy movies,
Real ale and real people.

I once interviewed him about his days at Rover for a play I was writing. He told many excellent stories which got absorbed into the show but I only used one direct quote (which, in deference to our location I am going to paraphrase). It was everyone's favourite line.

He described how, as a union activist, the bosses had sought to compromise him by offering him a management job. The chance of this promotion must have been enticing but it would have been against his principals and heaven knows, or at least is about to find out, how principled and stubborn Walter Suett is. His reply was firm and to the point: "You can't ride two horses with one back-side".

Walter knew which horse he was on and rode it to the end.
He died possessing very little, a man rich in humanity.
He was salt of the earth.
God Bless you Wal.
We miss you now and we always will.

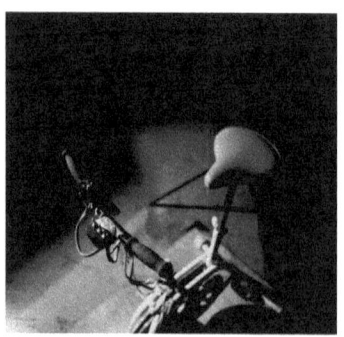
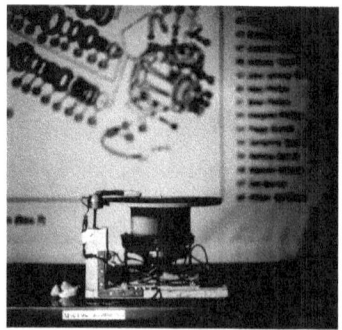

Griff's Story (full version)

This is a story from the future. It starts with Once Upon A Time, but for us it is a story about things that have yet to happen.

Once Upon A Time there was a King who had a problem. His kingdom had been rich and happy, but now people were coming to him complaining, "There is an invisible gas that is causing our children to wheeze and splutter," they said "and whilst we're at it," they added, "the winters are becoming terribly cold, whilst summers are too hot, spring is always too wet and the autumns are definitely too windy. What are you going to do about it?"

The King thought his subjects were spoilt and ungrateful but they kept complaining bitterly until he was forced to issue a proclamation. – *Whoever can rid this kingdom of its wheezing and foul weather may take my beautiful daughter's hand in marriage* – "what more can I do?" he muttered as he set off hunting.

Soon Princes were coming from far and wide, each fell in love with the King's beautiful daughter and each failed in the challenge. Years passed and the wheezing and weather got worse. Finally, when the people, and thus the king, were all in despair a young girl came to the palace and asked to speak with the King. "I wish to take up your challenge," she announced, to the King's astonishment. "Very well" he replied, doubtfully, "but listen, if you succeed you won't be marrying my beautiful daughter, understand?" the young girl said she understood and that she needed three things before she could complete the challenge. "Name them and they shall be yours," said the King immediately regretting his offer. "I will need a large factory, one year and all the diamonds in the kingdom," said the little girl with a smile.

The King was furious. "I can give you a factory and a year, but I cannot give you all the diamonds in my kingdom!" he roared. "Then I cannot help you," replied the girl who promptly turned on her heel and left the palace.

Now the people had heard about the young girl and were anxious to know what had come of her meeting with the King. When they learned of the enormous price she had demanded there was a huge argument. People without diamonds where happy with the price, those with diamonds were not. Those without diamonds accused those with diamonds of being selfish. Those with diamonds suggested those without diamonds buy their own if they were so anxious for them to be given away to small girls.

Just as the argument looked like breaking into a fight, a tall, elegant woman stepped forwards and spoke calmly "I have a beautiful diamond necklace and I would happily give it to the girl as I never wear it anymore. All the dances I used to attend are cancelled because of the foul weather. I love to dance and would happily dance without my necklace if the weather allowed it". On hearing this a short plump woman came forward. "I only have a small diamond, it is precious to me because it is part of my engagement ring, but it is not as precious as my son who coughs and wheezes to sleep every night. I would gladly trade my ring if it meant he could run around and play again". With this more people promised their diamonds until, eventually, even the King was shamed into promising to give the girl some of his smaller diamonds.

The next day the King reluctantly summoned the small girl back to his palace. "I cannot give you all the diamonds in the kingdom as you requested, but I can give you enough to make you the richest young girl in this or I venture any kingdom" with this the King poured a dazzling pile of jewels at the little girl's feet. The King expected the girl to be delighted, but instead she looked at the jewels with a sad face. "I know this should be as many diamonds as any girl could want" she sighed "but they are not enough for me. As I said at the start, I need all the diamonds in the kingdom". "This is madness!" the King ragged "Your price is far too high, people will call you greedy, hate you and try to steal from you". The little girl thought for a moment "I see that this is difficult for you, so we will strike a bargain. I still need all the diamonds in the kingdom, but I promise only to keep them for one year, at the end of this year they shall all be returned to their owners".

So all kingdom's diamonds were collected and given to the little girl, who took them in sacks to a big old factory on the edge of town where she started work. For a whole year no one was allowed into the factory and the girl never came out. Occasionally she asked for sandwiches to be delivered, for a ball of string or a hacksaw, but apart from this all was quiet and after a while people almost forgot about the small girl in the big factory. Then, as the year drew to its end, things changed, rumours started, people grew suspicious of the girl and were anxious to get their diamonds back.

On the last day of the year a huge crowd gathered at the factory gate. A small door opened in one of its vast green buildings and the little girl came out in her white plimsolls, white dress and play fairy wings. "Where are our diamonds?" The crowd shouted through the railings. "Open this gate, let us collect them!" "Your diamonds are all safe at the palace with The Keeper of the Kings Jewels" she smiled. Frantic with worry now the mob charged to the palace screaming and shouting, but The Keeper of the Kings Jewels was a huge and fierce man who wasn't to be intimidated. He made them all stand in an orderly queue and anyone who pushed was sent to the back. Eventually every last person had their diamonds returned to them, as good as new.

Everyone was so interested in the fate of the diamonds that it was some time before anyone asked about the challenge but eventually the little girl was summoned to the palace. "Well, we paid your price and gave you your factory, a year has passed and it seems to me you have failed in your challenge," rumbled the king, "I have a good mind to throw you in the dungeon!"

"Your highness" replied the girl, "I beg you not to throw me in your dungeon but first to listen to this lady" and with that a short plump woman wearing a diamond engagement ring stepped forward. "I don't know if it is this girl's doing," the woman started "but we live close to the factory and about six months ago I noticed my little boy was coughing and wheezing less and less, now he runs around and plays as happy as can be". "That's as maybe" said the king "but what about the weather? I can't see that has changed". With this a tall, elegant woman wearing a beautiful diamond necklace stepped forward "Of course it is difficult to spot patterns in the weather but last night we threw our New Year's Ball and for the first time in years all our guests arrived safely. I am sure this winter has been less harsh that those before it".

So with these and further tales the King was grudgingly satisfied that the Girl hadn't cheated him and had maybe even done some good. People had stopped moaning so much to him about the wheezing and the weather and all it had cost him was an old factory he didn't really need any more.

Everyone thought that was the unspectacular end of the story, but six months later there was a loud knock on the palace door. It was a furious headmaster holding the little Girl tight by her left ear and demanding to see the Keeper of the King's Jewels. The Keeper of the King's Jewels was told how the little girl had worn a large pair of diamond earrings to school that day, that they had been confiscated and now the Headteacher was searching for their rightful owner. The Keeper said no one had reported any missing jewels to him so he followed, with the King, as the Headteacher marched the girl to the Police Station. The Chief of Police said he had no reports of missing earrings. So he followed with his deputy as the little girl was marched to her factory and forced to unlock the gates.

Inside the illustrious crowd wandered around, unsure where to go or what they were looking for. Eventually the King came to the biggest building in the factory, pulled open its huge sliding door, let out a high-pitched scream and fainted. The Chief of Police grabbed the girl and said "Right girl, you're coming with me" but no one else moved or said anything. Inside the building it was dark, despite the wide open door, and holes cut in the ceiling and walls. In the darkness, sparkling like a million stars were all the diamonds the Girl was supposed to have returned to their owners six months ago.

"Let me explain," cried the girl wriggling free of the Chief of Police's grasp, "let me show you how it works," and so she took the astonished crowd on a tour. She showed them how thousands of engagement rings focussed all the sunlight that entered the room down into bracelets that in turn reflected and refracted light in and out of rainbows and how this light was combined, using necklaces and pendants strung across the building on string, in towards a central point where the King's biggest ceremonial diamonds sat, held in rusty old school science stands, alongside the biggest diamonds from the Lords of Industry and those from banks and corporate strong rooms. These large stones each focussed the light into a small black box.

"Don't look in there!" shouted the girl as the deputy chief of police leaned forward to inspect the box, "it's too bright, it will blind you". "I don't understand," the Keeper of the King's Jewels scratched his head, "I thought we had returned all these diamonds".

"We returned all the original diamonds," said the girl "Each night I smuggled out a bag for you to take care of it was because I had already made their replacements. I made all the diamonds you see here, they are brand new." And sure enough, wearing welding goggles, it was clear to see that in the black box, very slowly, at the centre of the smallest brightest blaze of light imaginable, the little girl was making diamonds.

Every daylight hour the factory was sucking in the invisible gas and breathing out pure oxygen. Each diamond was a permanent carbon store highly compressed, a museum containing carbon from the Great Fire Of London, Oil Fires in the Gulf, forest fires in Australia, exhaust from school runs and Grand Prix races, Hitler's breath, Martin Luther King and Olympic Rowers, choirs singing, homes being heated, airplanes crossing the sky, whatever you care to imagine, each clear glinting stone held its trace.

The King, the Headteacher, the keeper of the King's Jewels, the deputy and chief of Police and the little girl's granddad stood amazed, their jaws slack, dribbling slightly not knowing what to say or do.

Gill has two ends to the story. In one the price of diamonds plummets until a mysterious explosion at the factory blows the girl and all her diamonds into the air where they are lost to scavengers and the rubble. Tonight he chooses the happy ending, in which the price of diamonds plummets and over time everyone comes to wear them and glittering buildings are bejewelled in them and the whole kingdom sparkles in a host of rainbows as a gentle rain falls the through clean air of tranquil sunsets.

About the illustration and design

The illustrations for the covers of these books were undertaken by students at Birmingham City University as the final module of their first-year illustration course during the Spring/Summer of 2018. The images were developed through workshops using variations of the theatre-devising methods employed by Stan's Cafe but adapted and applied to the making of visual work. The resulting work was shown in the pop-up exhibition *The Something Of Somebody Something* at Stan's Cafe's venue @AE Harris in May 2018.

The design concept of the books was produced by final year Graphic Design student Aimee Chapman. These were then further developed for print in a collaborative process between Stan's Cafe and the University's Innovation Product Support Service (IPSS) which involved helping the company to select appropriate DTP software, undertaking training and selecting a suitable print on demand service.

Gareth Courage
Lecturer in Illustration
Birmingham City University

www.ingramcontent.com/pod-product-compliance
Lightning Source LLC
Chambersburg PA
CBHW071756080526
44588CB00013B/2270